Totally COOL Nails

50 FUN AND EASY NAIL ART DESIGNS
for Kids

CATHERINE RODGERS

Creator of the YouTube channel
~ TotallyCoolNails ~

Adamsmedia
Avon, Massachusetts

Published by
Adams Media, a division of F+W Media, Inc.
57 Littlefield Street, Avon, MA 02322. U.S.A.
www.adamsmedia.com

ISBN 10: 1-4405-7241-0
ISBN 13: 978-1-4405-7241-8
eISBN 10: 1-4405-7242-9
eISBN 13: 978-1-4405-7242-5

Printed by RR Donnelley, Roanoke, VA, U.S.A.
10 9 8 7 6 5 4 3 2 1
January 2014

Library of Congress Cataloging-in-Publication Data

Rodgers, Catherine.
   Totally cool nails / Catherine Rodgers, creator of the YouTube channel TotallyCoolNails.
       pages cm
   Audience: Grades 4 to 7.
   Includes bibliographical references.
   ISBN 978-1-4405-7241-8 (pb : alk. paper) – ISBN 1-4405-7241-0 (pb : alk. paper) – ISBN 978-1-4405-7242-5 (ebook) – ISBN 1-4405-7242-9 (ebook)
1. Nail art (Manicuring)–Juvenile literature. I. Title.
   TT958.3.R633 2014
   646.7'27–dc23
                                     2013044599

Readers are urged to take all appropriate precautions before undertaking any how-to task. Always read and follow instructions and safety warnings for all tools and materials, and call in a professional if the task stretches your abilities too far. Although every effort has been made to provide the best possible information in this book, neither the publisher nor the author is responsible for accidents, injuries, or damage incurred as a result of tasks undertaken by readers. This book is not a substitute for professional services.

Many of the designations used by manufacturers and sellers to distinguish their products are claimed as trademarks. Where those designations appear in this book and F+W Media, Inc. was aware of a trademark claim, the designations have been printed with initial capital letters.

Photographs by Home Town Photo.

This book is available at quantity discounts for bulk purchases.
For information, please call 1-800-289-0963.

CONTENTS

3

INTRODUCTION

You would give anything to copy your favorite celebrity's nails or be able to recreate the nail art from that awesome tutorial you saw on YouTube, but you're not really sure it's possible to get that same look. Creating totally cool nail art designs is not only fun, but incredibly easy with just a few simple tools and tricks. Inside this book, you'll not only learn all about the basics of creating nail art, but you'll also discover how to paint everything from simple polka dots to an adorable panda—in just a few steps!

The most important thing to remember, though, is that practice makes perfect. When you're first starting out, getting your design to look exactly like the picture can be super tricky, but don't give up! If you take your time through each of the steps listed in this book, you'll become a pro in no time. You can also ask a parent or friend for help if you're having a hard time with a particular design. Who knows, maybe they'll even give you some great ideas for creating your very own nail art.

So say goodbye to boring nails and hello to fabulous nail art designs! With this book, you'll have everything you need to make your nails sparkle and create fun, one-of-a-kind designs.

CHAPTER 1

How to Use This Book

You might think that manicurists are the only ones who can create amazing nail designs. After all, they've taken classes and have given millions of people who've visited their salons perfect manicures. But designing your nails isn't nearly as scary or difficult as you might think. In fact, once you get started, you'll wonder why you were so afraid to paint your own nails in the first place. Best of all, you'll proudly show off your designs to friends and family, knowing that you created this celebrity-approved look all on your own! There are just a couple of things you need to know before you get started.

PREPPING YOUR NAILS AND TAKING CARE OF YOUR DESIGN

Creating the perfect nail art design isn't just about bright colors or funky patterns. You have to give each nail a chance to dry before you go on to the next step in order to make the design last. You also have to make sure that your nails are in good shape. It might seem like a lot of work and time to get just the right look, but it'll be worth it, I promise. Your nails will not only stay healthy and clean, but you'll also keep your design looking super pretty for much, much longer. Now, who wouldn't want that?

Cutting and Shaping Your Nails

Now, this next part might be a little tricky, so you may want to ask your parents or a friend for help. Before you start any design, wipe your nails with a cotton ball soaked in nail polish remover. Even if your nails aren't painted, you should always make this your first step because it helps the nail polish stick to your nails. Then take a nail file or emery board and file your nails into one of the five common nail shapes: oval, square, pointed, squoval, or round. Your parents may already know what shape works best for your hands, but if they don't, you can do a simple Internet search together to figure out which shape works best for you. Finally, have your parents trim any hangnails around your nails with a pair of nail clippers. You should also apply a moisturizer after you've completed your filing and clipping to help keep your nails looking this way.

These simple steps will make your nails look sparkly clean and give you the start you need to create beautiful nail art.

Base Coat and Top Coat

A base and top coat can also make your nail art look like it was done by a pro. These two clear nail polishes will give you a smooth canvas to work on and seal in your design. They are sold under many different brands and range from strengthening to nonstaining types. While your design will look just as good without these two special nail polishes, using them will give both your natural nail and your nail art the best possible protection against stains and chips.

After you've prepared your nails, the first nail polish you should use is the base coat. A base coat fills in lines and cracks on your nails, so your nail color can easily slide onto your nails. This will not only make your nail art design last longer, but will also keep the nail polish color from staining your natural nail. Like the base coat, a top coat polish is clear and protects your nail. Applied after you finish your nail art design, the top coat seals it in and prevents the color from fading. It also adds shine to the look, and when it is reapplied during the week, it will help prevent chipping. When applying a top coat, make sure to paint underneath your tips as well, since this makes the nail art design last much longer.

TOOLS AND TECHNIQUES

While every piece of nail art is different, there are a few things you should keep on hand when you're creating a design. Your go-to nail art kit should include a dotting tool, a nail art brush, the nail colors you're using, and a cosmetic wedge. These tools are very inexpensive and can be found in beauty supply stores and online at websites like *www. amazon.com*. For nail color, any brand will do as long as it coats your nail well. However, if you don't have one of these tools, it's easy to be creative with items you have around your house. No matter what tool you use, be sure to clean it with nail polish remover after you finish the design in order to get a clean look every time.

Dotting Tool

A dotting tool makes the perfect beginner's tool and is definitely something you need to put on your wish list! It has a long handle with a small round ball at each tip (some dotting tools will only have one tip). As you can probably guess by the name, dotting tools are used to create dots, but that doesn't mean that your nail art has to be simple or boring. You can use the dotting tool to create flowers or even a starry sky. To use a dotting tool, simply drip some nail polish onto a piece of paper, dip the tool in it, and dot your nail. The key here is to coat the ball at the top of the tool with just enough nail color to create the right size of dot—the more you add, the bigger your dot will be. If you need to create small dots but can't find a dotting tool, you can use a toothpick or even the rounded end of a bobby pin. For larger dots, the end of a paintbrush or makeup brush handle both work well.

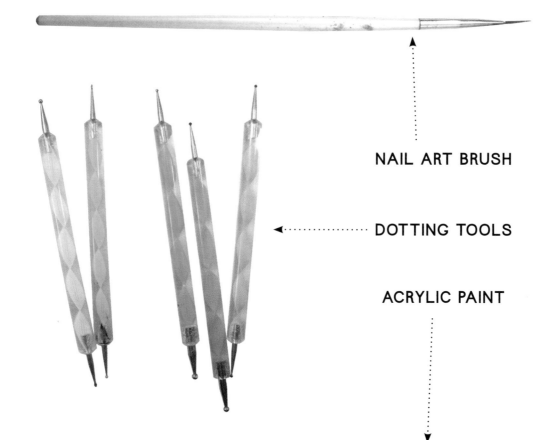

NAIL ART BRUSH

DOTTING TOOLS

ACRYLIC PAINT

Nail Art Brush

The nail art brush is another tool that you'll want to get, since it gives you more control over your design. There are a variety of styles and sizes, so make sure you consider what type of art you want to create before buying one. If you're still not sure what kind of brush you'll need, many stores offer a nail art brush kit that comes with a selection of brushes in various shapes and sizes. For the nail art in this book, however, I'd recommend sticking to a thin brush with fine bristles. This brush, sometimes called a detailing brush, is great for small hands and fingernails. It also makes it easier to draw straight lines, but it will take some time to get used to if you don't have a steady hand. If you have a hard time holding the brush, moving the hand you are working on instead of the hand you are painting with will help you create straight lines. To use a detailing brush, place drops of nail polish on a piece of paper, dip the tip of the brush into the nail polish, and paint a design on your nails just like you would with a paintbrush. Be careful to never dip the nail art brush into the nail polish bottle, though, as this can create unwanted drips and messy designs. If you don't have a nail art brush, you can use a small makeup brush or a small paintbrush instead. If you're using a paintbrush, however, ask your parents to trim the bristles down to the right shape and size for your design. You should always make sure to clean your brushes in between steps in order to make them last longer and create a clean design. To do this, you can dip the brushes in pure acetone nail polish remover and wipe the tips off with a dry paper towel. If you're using acrylic paint for your nail art designs, you can clean the brushes by simply rinsing the tips in lukewarm water.

Acrylic Paint

You've probably used acrylic paint before—it's the kind of paint a lot of people use for their arts-and-crafts projects. While it may seem like a weird idea, manicurists have been using acrylic paint for nail art designs for years. Since acrylic paint can be mixed to create a variety of different colors, it is cheaper than using regular nail polish and can help you add details without having to own a huge nail-polish collection. It is also a great beginner's tool because it can easily be wiped away if a mistake is made before it dries. When using acrylic paint, you should always apply a base coat and a nail color first. The paint will only be used to add details and will not give you the same shimmery color that nail polish does.

CHAPTER 2

Nail Art Designs

American Flag Nails

What's not to love about the Fourth of July? Watching fireworks and eating all the yummy foods at cookouts are always a ton of fun and what make this holiday so great. With this all-American design, you can find your own special way to celebrate the country!

1 Start by painting your thumb and index-finger nails with a blue nail polish. Then paint the rest of your nails with a red nail polish.

2 Dip a dotting tool into white polish and place a few dots in a polka-dot pattern on the blue nails.

3 Using a nail art brush and white nail polish, create stripes by painting thick horizontal lines onto the red nails.

4 Finally, apply a top coat to your nails to seal in the design.

Balloon Nails

If you're an adventurer or dream of traveling the globe one day, you'll love this design! Sure, it may not help you make your house float off to a faraway land, but this cute red balloon will remind you that there is still a whole world out there for you to explore.

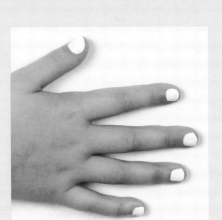

1 Start by painting your nails with a white nail polish.

2 On a cosmetic wedge, paint a wide stripe of light-blue polish next to a stripe of white nail polish. Dab the cosmetic wedge onto each nail, keeping the light blue at the cuticle to form a gradient. A gradient is just when the darker color fades into the lighter color. You may need to reapply the nail polish between nails to make the color more vibrant.

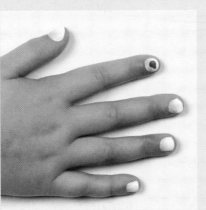

3 Using the nail art brush and red nail polish, create an oval on your index-finger nail and fill it in. This will be your balloon for the design.

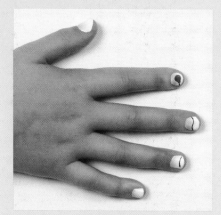

4 Using a nail art brush and black nail polish, create a thin, wavy line across your index-, middle-, and ring-finger nails, making sure that the line stays connected between all nails. This wavy line will form the balloon string.

5 Finally, apply a top coat to your nails to seal in the design.

Bow Nails

Simple and sweet, this bow nail art is great for every day! You can wear this design just about anywhere, from school to a friend's birthday party. You can even switch up the colors in the design to match your favorite outfit or the month's big holiday, like using green nail polish instead of turquoise for an easy St. Patrick's Day-inspired design.

1 Start by painting your nails with a turquoise nail polish.

2 Using a dotting tool and white nail polish, place a few dots in a polka-dot pattern on all of your nails except the ring-finger nails.

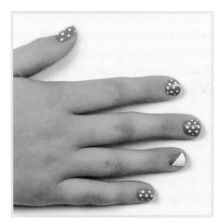

3 Using a nail art brush and the white nail polish, draw a diagonal line from the leftmost corner of your nail to the rightmost corner. Fill in the bottom section with white nail polish.

4 Using the dotting tool and turquoise nail polish, place a few dots in a polka-dot pattern inside the white area.

5 Using the nail art brush and black nail polish, draw a diagonal line over the original line you drew.

6 Using the nail art brush and black nail polish, draw an X in the center of the black line and close up the sides of the X by drawing one small vertical line on each side. Fill in the triangles with black nail polish. This will create a bow on your ring-finger nails.

7 Finally, apply a top coat to your nails to seal in the design.

Bow and Leopard Nails

This nail art design is the spunky cousin of the Bow Nails. You still get the adorable little bow from the original nail art that you love, but you also get some really cool spots! So wear your leopard print proudly, because this design is sure to get you noticed—even if you don't let out a mighty roar!

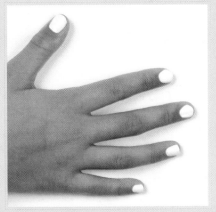

1 Start by painting your nails with a white nail poli[sh].

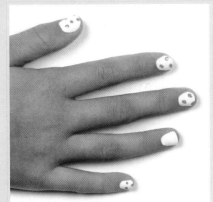

2 Using a dotting tool and pink nail polish, place several random dots on all of your nails except the ring-finger nails. Don't worry about the dots being perfectly round; a leopard's spots are slightly irregular.

3 Using a nail art brush or a toothpick and black nail polish, draw C shapes around the edges of the dots.

4 Using the nail art brush and pink nail polish, draw an X on your ring finger and close up the sides of the X by drawing one small vertical line on each side. Fill in the triangles with pink nail polish. This will create a bow on your ring-finger nails.

5 Using a nail art brush and black nail polish, place a small X in the center of the bow.

6 Using a dotting tool and light-pink nail polish, place a dot in the center of the bow.

7 Finally, apply a top coat to your nails to seal in the design.

Braided Nails

Braids are all the rage when it comes to styling your hair, so why not wear them on your nails, too? This funky design uses three awesome colors to copy those fun braids you see in many girls' hair—maybe your own as well. Easy yet super stylish, this nail art will have all your friends wondering how you got to be such a fashionista!

1 Start by painting your nails with a silver nail polish.

2 Using a nail art brush and light-blue nail polish, draw a thick diagonal line from the leftmost corner of your nail to the center of your nail.

3 Using the nail art brush and light-pink nail polish, draw a thick diagonal line from the rightmost corner of your nail to the center of your nail. This line should meet the light-blue line.

4 Using the nail art brush and the light-blue nail polish, draw another thick diagonal line right underneath the pink one you just created.

5 Using the nail art brush and light-pink nail polish, draw a thick diagonal line from the left side of your nail to the center of your nail. This line should meet the light-blue line you just created.

6 Finally, apply a top coat to your nails to seal in the design.

Butterfly Nails

These itty-bitty butterflies may be the cutest thing ever! Their brightly colored wings flutter from nail to nail and will remind you of the spring, when you'll catch a glimpse of them flying from flower to flower.

1 Start by painting your nails with a light-yellow nail polish.

2 Using a dotting tool and pink nail polish, place two larger dots side by side on your nails, and then just below that, two slightly smaller dots. This will create the butterfly's wings.

3 Repeat Step 2 using purple and blue nail polishes.

4 Using a nail art brush and black nail polish, draw a thin line in between the two large dots down to the smaller ones. This thin line will turn into the butterfly's body.

5 Using the nail art brush and black nail polish, draw thin, curly lines coming out from the top of the body. These will become the butterfly's antennae.

6 Finally, apply a top coat to your nails to seal in the design.

Circle Circle, Dot Dot Nails

Don't worry, this awesome design is cootie-free, but that doesn't mean you won't still get plenty of attention! The awesome circles and dots only take a few minutes to create, but all your friends will want to see your nails again and again just to try to figure out how you did it.

1 Start by painting your nails with a light-pink nail polish.

2 Using a dotting tool and blue, green, or white nail polish, create one or two large dots on each nail.

3 Using a dotting tool and a nail polish color you haven't used, create a small dot in the center of the larger ones.

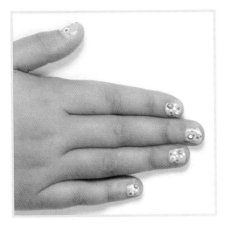

4 Using a dotting tool and blue, green, and white nail polish, create tiny dots going around the large dots on each of your nails.

5 Finally, apply a top coat to your nails to seal in the design.

Color Block Nails

Color blocking is another design pattern you may have worn or seen your friends and family wear. It may look hard to copy, but it's really not if you just think of the design as a bunch of simple rectangles. They're the same ones you learned about in math class, just way more cool.

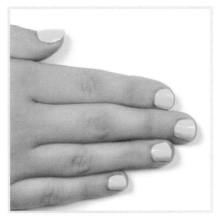

1 Start by painting your nails with a yellow nail po

2 Using a nail art brush and black nail polish, draw rectangular shapes on each nail.

3 Using a nail art brush and pink and blue nail polish, fill in each rectangle with a different color.

4 Finally, apply a top coat to your nails to seal in the design.

Splatter Nails

If you've ever dreamed of getting covered in bright-colored slime during some of your favorite award shows, then this fun design is for you! Best of all, you'll get to show off your gooey goop without ever having to clean up any of the mess.

1 Start by painting your nails with a yellow nail polish.

2 Dip a large dotting tool into blue polish and place two or three dots close to the tip of each nail. Drag the blue color toward the tip of the nail.

3 Fill in the tip area with the blue to connect all of the dripping areas.

4 Finally, apply a top coat to your nails to seal in the design.

Faded Dots Nails

If you say "abraca-dabra," the dots in the design will start to disappear! Well, they won't disappear, but they'll sure look like it! The different-size dots in this design trick the eye into seeing the dots fading or slowly disappearing from sight. The best part? You won't actually need magic to create these fantastic nails, because they're just that easy!

1 Start by painting your nails with a dark-purple nail polish.

2 Using a dotting tool and white nail polish, create three large dots along the tip of the nail, leaving some space in between.

3 Using the same dotting tool and nail polish, create medium-size dots above the larger ones.

4 Using the same dotting tool and nail polish, create small dots above the medium ones.

5 Finally, apply a top coat to your nails to seal in the design.

Faded Hot-Pink Zebra Nails

Looking for something fun and wild? Then this design is for you! Taking animal print to a whole new world, this zebra-inspired nail art design will get you noticed with its awesome pattern and bright-pink color!

1 Start by painting your nails with a white nail polish.

2 On a cosmetic wedge, paint a wide stripe of pink nail polish next to a stripe of white nail polish. Dab the cosmetic wedge at an angle onto each nail, so that the pink begins at the top corner and forms a gradient. You may need to reapply the nail polish between nails to make the color more vibrant.

3 Using a nail art brush and black nail polish, draw wavy lines on the white part of the nail. Make sure that there are lines that start on each side of your nail.

4 Finally, apply a top coat to your nails to seal in the design.

Frog Nails

Ribbit, ribbit! Even though this design is super easy to create, it will call for attention no matter where you go. So forget what you heard about frogs being slimy and gross—the one in this nail art will show you that they can be oh-so-cute and even more fun to show off!

1 Start by painting your ring-finger nails with a light-yellow nail polish. Then paint the rest of your nails with a hot-pink nail polish.

2 Using a nail art brush and a lime-green nail polish, create a half circle at the tip of the ring-finger nail.

3 Using a dotting tool and the lime-green nail polish, place two dots just above the half circle.

4 Using a dotting tool and black nail polish, place two tiny dots inside the green ones to create the frog's eyes. Place two more tiny dots just below the eyes to create his nose.

5 Using a nail art brush, create the frog's mouth by drawing a U shape at the tip of your nail.

6 Finally, apply a top coat to your nails to seal in the design.

Funky Dots Nails

Travel back in time with this groovy design! With just a couple of bright colors and a few super cool dots, you'll take your nails into the '70s with this retro-inspired nail art.

1 Start by painting your nails with an orange nail polish.

2 Using a dotting tool and dark-purple and blue nail polishes, place rows of dots on each nail, alternating between colors.

3 Using the same dotting tool, place a smaller dot on top of the ones you created. Make sure that the smaller dot is the opposite color, so if you have a medium-size dark-purple dot, the smaller dot should be blue.

4 Finally, apply a top coat to your nails to seal in the design.

Heart Nails

Why stick to just one heart when you can wear a bunch? You can create this design using your favorite colors for the hearts, or you could use festive colors to celebrate a holiday or the changing of the seasons. Since we used leaf colors to create our hearts, the pictured nail art would be a great way to show off your love for fall!

1 Start by painting your nails with a white nail polish.

2 Using a nail art brush and several different nail polish colors, create V shapes all over your nails.

3 Using the same nail art brush and colors, draw an M on top of each V shape to complete your heart. Fill in the hearts with the nail polish color you used to draw its outline.

4 Finally, apply a top coat to your nails to seal in the design.

Ice Cream Nails

This summertime treat looks just as good on your nails! Unlike an ice cream truck, you won't have to follow this design around forever to get your very own cone. Its bright colors and fun dots are super easy to pull off and when you're finished, you'll feel a lot like you do when the ice cream man has finally pulled into your neighborhood.

1 Start by painting your nails with a pale-yellow nail polish.

2 Using a dotting tool and pink and blue nail polishes, randomly place small dots on your nails, starting from the tip of the nail and fading toward the cuticle. Leave your ring-finger nails blank.

3 On the ring-finger nail, create a triangle using a nail art brush and brown nail polish.

4 Using a dotting tool and pink nail polish, place a large dot just above the triangle.

5 Using the dotting tool and pink nail polish, place one smaller dot on each side of the larger one you created.

6 Finally, apply a top coat to your nails to seal in the design.

Mustache Nails

So I mustache you a question: How cute is this nail art design? It takes the popular mustache trend to the next level with fun colors that are sure to catch your friend's eye!

1 Start by painting each of your nails with brightly colored nail polishes. Each nail should be a different color from the rest.

2 Using a dotting tool and a brightly colored nail polish, place two dots right next to each other at the center of your nail. Make sure that the nail polish color is different from your base nail polish color.

3 Using the dotting tool and the same nail polish color, place smaller dots on either side of the larger dots.

4 Finally, apply a top coat to your nails to seal in the design.

Ombre Dot Nails

The hot hair trend isn't just for your head anymore—your nails can pull off the ombre look, too! This design uses three different shades of pink to get that popular ombre effect and make the dots look like they're getting lighter. Be sure to choose shades of pink that are only a tiny bit different than each other for the best outcome.

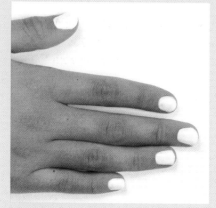

1 Start by painting your nails with a white nail polish.

2 Using a dotting tool and a light-pink nail polish, place two rows of dots at the top of your nail.

3 Using the dotting tool and a medium-pink nail polish, place two more rows of dots below the previous rows.

4 Using the dotting tool and a dark-pink nail polish, place a few more rows of dots below the previous rows. The longer your nails are, the more rows you will be able to fit.

5 Finally, apply a top coat to your nails to seal in the design.

Panda Nails

This adorable nail art design will show you why these cuddly pandas are the stars of any zoo! You can wear their cute faces on your nails to show off your love for the fuzzy animal everywhere you go.

1 Start by painting your nails with a light-blue nail polish.

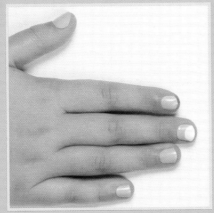

2 Using a nail art brush and white nail polish, create a half circle toward the tip of your middle-finger nail.

3 Using a dotting tool and black nail polish, place two large dots inside the half circle. These will be your panda's eyes.

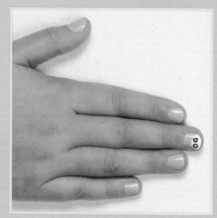

4 Using a dotting tool and white nail polish, place a small dot in the large black dots for his eyes.

5 Using the dotting tool and black nail polish, place a small dot below the eyes for his nose.

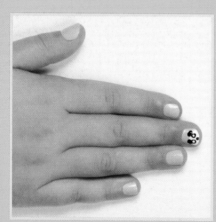

6 Using a nail art brush and black nail polish, create two smaller half circles on either side of the white half circle for his ears.

7 Finally, apply a top coat to your nails to seal in the design.

Plaid Nails

Don't worry—you don't have to go to a private school to pull off these cool nails! Since plaid is a pattern that never goes out of style, this trendy nail design is perfect for any time of year! While we love the colors shown here, you can always replace them with your favorite shades or pick colors that match your snazziest outfit!

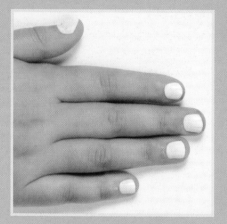

1 Start by painting your nails with a white nail polish.

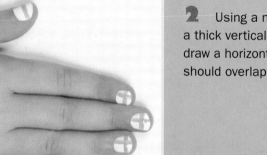

2 Using a nail art brush and hot-pink nail polish, draw a thick vertical line on the rightmost side of your nail. Then draw a horizontal line at the tip of your nail. These two lines should overlap.

3 Using the nail art brush and a dark-purple nail polish, draw a medium-width line over the pink lines you just created.

4 Using the nail art brush and a medium-blue nail polish, draw a thin vertical line on the leftmost side of your nail. Then draw a horizontal line at the top of your nail. These two lines should overlap.

5 Finally, apply a top coat to your nails to seal in the design.

Rainbow Dots Nails

If you're looking for a quick pop of color to brighten up your day, then look no further! This cute and colorful nail design will only take a few minutes to create, but will leave you smiling all day with its bright rainbow pattern.

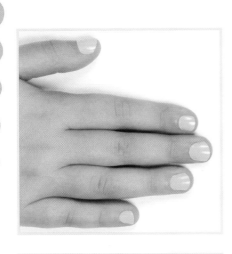

1 Start by painting your nails with a light-pink nail polish.

2 Using a dotting tool and a red nail polish, place one row of dots near the cuticle of your nail. This row does not need to be straight.

3 Repeat Step 2 with orange, yellow, green, blue, and purple nail polishes. Be sure to place each new row underneath the one that was just created.

4 Finally, apply a top coat to your nails to seal in the design.

Rainbow Bubbles Nails

Get ready to be tackled by your friends when you wear this rainbow design! So simple yet incredibly awesome, these bubbles will leave your pals wondering just how you did it. It's totally up to you whether you keep them guessing or reveal your secret about this polka-dot design.

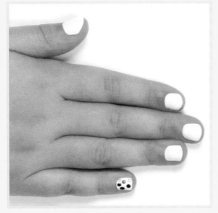

1 Start by painting your nails with a white nail polish.

2 Using a dotting tool and purple nail polish, place a vertical row of dots on your pinky-finger nail. Create another row of dots on your pinky-finger nail by using the dotting tool and blue nail polish.

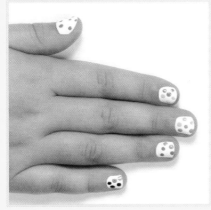

3 Repeat Step 2 using blue, green, yellow, orange, and red nail polishes. Each nail should include just two colors and follow a rainbow pattern.

4 Using the dotting tool and white nail polish, place a small dot inside all of the colored dots.

5 Finally, apply a top coat to your nails to seal in the design.

Rainbow Stripes Nails

Who doesn't love stripes? With this design, you can use the colors of the rainbow and thick lines to really make your nails pop! The trick to recreating these straight lines is to use really thin pieces of tape, which you can find at any beauty supply store. It'll not only guide you as you apply your favorite nail polish colors, but it'll also make sure that that little white line peeks through when you're done.

1 Start by painting your nails with a white nail polish.

2 Using tape, separate each nail into three vertical sections.

3 Using a nail art brush and pink, purple, blue, green, yellow, orange, and red nail polishes, paint each section a different color of the rainbow. You can fill each nail in according to the traditional rainbow pattern or switch them up.

4 Carefully remove the tape and apply a top coat to your nails to seal in the design.

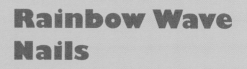

Rainbow Wave Nails

This bold rainbow nail art design will definitely catch some eyes! Its wave shape makes it a super cool version of the rainbow you've been drawing all these years. And best of all, you don't have to worry about how straight your lines are since each color should look like it's moving around, kind of like how a flag would wave in the wind.

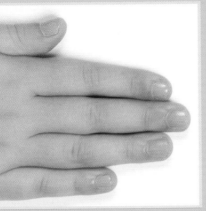

1 Start by painting your nails with a light-pink nail polish.

2 Using a dotting tool and orange nail polish, place several dots in a row near the cuticle. Make sure you leave some of the pink just above it.

3 Repeat Step 2 using the remaining colors of the rainbow: yellow, green, blue, and purple, making sure that each new row is stacked below the previous one.

4 Finally, apply a top coat to your nails to seal in the design.

Daisy Nails

Celebrate the start of spring with these pretty flowers! A splash of hot-pink nail polish and bright white daisies are all you need to remind you of the season and all the plants that are springing up from the ground.

1 Start by painting your nails with a hot-pink nail polish.

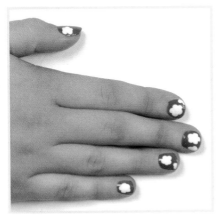

2 Using a dotting tool and white nail polish, place five dots close together in a circle on each of your nails. If you'd like to create a bunch of daisies, repeat this step on different areas of your nail.

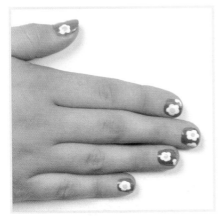

3 Using the same dotting tool and yellow nail polish, place one dot in the center of the white dots. This completes your daisy.

4 Finally, apply a top coat to your nails to seal in the design.

Snowflake Nails

When the cold winter air begins to rush in and the holidays are just around the corner, there's no better way to welcome in the season than with this cool nail art design! You'll have a great time creating your very own blizzard!

1 Start by painting your nails with a dark-blue nail polish.

2 Using a nail art brush and white nail polish, draw an X on the nail to begin the snowflake. If you'd like to create a blizzard on your nails, repeat this step on different areas of your nail.

3 Using the same tools, draw a line that intersects the X.

4 Using the same tools, create a V toward the end of each line, making sure that each V is divided by part of the line.

5 Finally, apply a top coat to your nails to seal in the design.

Starfish Nails

School's out, and now it's time to catch some sun! What better way to start your summer than by painting your nails with the adorable starfish in this sea-inspired design?

1 Start by painting your nails with a light-blue nail polish.

2 On a cosmetic wedge, paint a wide stripe of light-blue polish next to a stripe of darker blue nail polish. Dab the cosmetic wedge onto each nail, keeping the light blue at the cuticle to form a gradient. You may need to reapply the nail polish between nails to make the color more vibrant.

3 Using a small nail art brush and yellow nail polish, draw a small star on your nails. Make sure you start with thin lines and then color in the shape once you're happy with how your star came out.

4 Using a small dotting tool or toothpick and white nail polish, place dots along each star's tips and in their centers.

5 Finally, apply a top coat to your nails to seal in the design.

St. Patrick's Day Nails

Forget those boring green shirts and have some fun this St. Patrick's Day with this awesome nail art design! Inspired by the well-known clover of the holiday, this design may just lead you to a pot of gold!

1 Start by painting your nails with a medium-green nail polish.

2 Using a nail art brush and dark-green nail polish, paint three little heart shapes that attach at their tips on your ring-finger nail.

3 On the rest of your nails, paint ⅓ of each nail with a gold nail polish.

4 Using the same tools that you used for the clover, draw a line under the hearts for the clover's stem. With a dotting tool and gold nail polish, make a dot in the center of the clover.

5 Finally, apply a top coat to your nails to seal in the design.

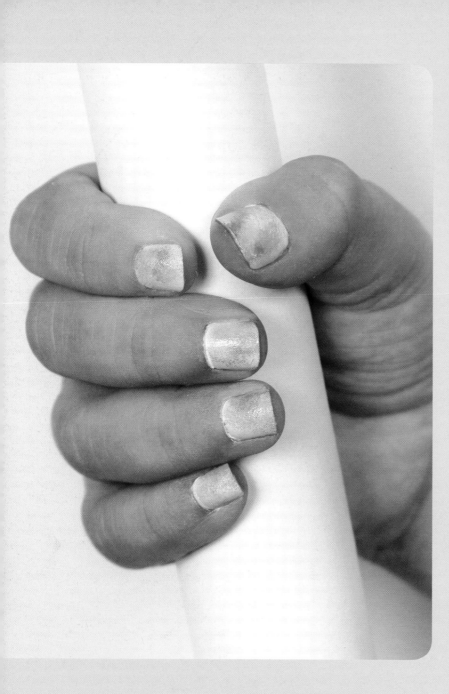

Watercolor Nails

Do you love to paint or look at all the artwork hanging up on museum walls? With this design, you can bring out your inner artist! After painting a splash of color here and a splash of color there, you'll create a masterpiece on your nails that you'll really love showing off!

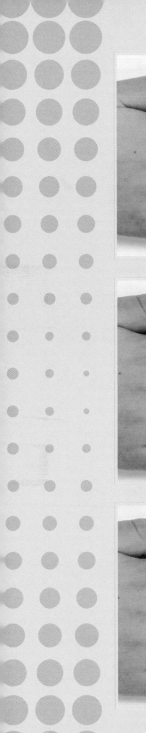

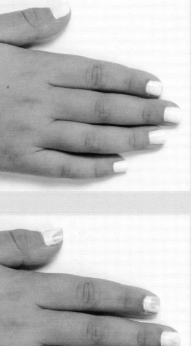

1 Start by painting your nails with a white nail polish.

2 Using a small piece of a cosmetic wedge and some tweezers, apply a blue nail polish to a small section of your nails.

3 Repeat Step 2 using pink and yellow, or whatever colors you'd like, on different sections of your nail.

4 Once the white is filled in with color, apply a top coat to your nails to seal in the design.

Bunny Nails

What could be better than an adorable bunny hopping around on your nails? Maybe a bunny hopping around, eating some yummy carrots? Well, that's what you get here! Wear this totally cute design for Easter or whenever you need to add an extra boost of cuteness to your day!

1 Start by painting your nails with a light-blue nail polish.

2 Using a nail art brush and white nail polish, create a half circle on the tip of your middle-finger nail.

3 Using the same tools, draw two long oval shapes above the half circle. These will become your bunny's ears.

4 Using a nail art brush and pink nail polish, draw a smaller oval inside each of the white ovals.

5 Using a dotting tool and black nail polish, place two small dots near the top of the half circle for the bunny's eyes.

6 Using the dotting tool and pink nail polish, place a dot in the center of the half circle for the nose.

7 Using a nail art brush and black nail polish, draw short, diagonal lines on the sides of the nose for whiskers and two curved lines attached to the nose for the bunny's mouth.

8 Using a nail art brush and orange nail polish, create long oval shapes on the rest of the nails. Fill in each orange oval. Use green nail polish to create M shapes above the ovals and fill in the leaves of the carrots.

9 Finally, apply a top coat to your nails to seal in the design.

Butterfly Wing Nails

Butterfly wings are so mesmerizing and will capture your attention even from a distance. With this pretty design, you'll copy the monarch butterfly's wing pattern and draw all of your friends' attention to your awesome nails!

1 Start by painting your nails with a yellow nail polish.

2 On a cosmetic wedge, paint a wide stripe of yellow polish next to a stripe of orange nail polish. Dab the cosmetic wedge onto each nail, keeping the yellow at the cuticle to form a gradient. You may need to reapply the nail polish between nails to make the color more vibrant.

3 Using a nail art brush and black nail polish, create a curved line at the top of your nail and a much thicker one toward the bottom of your nail.

4 Fill in the area below the bottom line with black nail polish.

5 Using a nail art brush and black nail polish, draw three curved lines connecting the top line with the bottom line.

6 Using a dotting tool and white nail polish, place dots in the bottom black area.

7 Finally, apply a top coat to your nails to seal in the design.

Candy Cane Nails

When the weather starts getting chilly, you know the winter holidays are just around the corner. That means yummy hot cocoa, snuggling up in your PJs with friends and family, and of course, those bright-red candy canes! This fun design stars those famous candy cane stripes that you love, and while you can't take a bite out of it, you'll definitely add a touch of sweetness to your day!

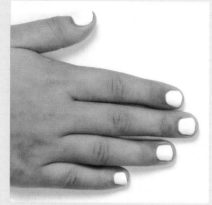

1 Start by painting your nails with a white nail polish.

2 Using a nail art brush and red nail polish, draw diagonal lines on each nail, making sure that some lines are super thin and others are thicker, so that your design resembles a candy cane.

3 Finally, apply a top coat to your nails to seal in the design.

Candy Heart Nails

Forget valentines and flowers! Everyone knows that the best part about Valentine's Day is getting that box of yummy heart-shaped candies. The colorful hearts in this design will make your friends say, "Be Mine" and wonder how you got such candy-sweet nails.

1 Start by painting your nails with a hot-pink nail polish.

2 Using several different shades of pastel colors and a small nail art brush, begin creating V shapes on all of the nails. Top each V shape with an M shape, so that it looks more like a candy heart. If you're using acrylic paint, you can create pastel colors by mixing your favorite shades with white paint. Use the same color to paint the insides of the hearts.

3 Finally, apply a top coat to your nails to seal in the design.

Confetti Nails

Get ready to celebrate! With this design, you'll have a ton of fun no matter what day it is. Great for wearing to birthday parties, New Year's celebrations, or just because it's Friday, you'll always find some reason to have a ball with this festive confetti design!

1 Start by painting your nails with a light-pink nail polish.

2 Using a nail art brush and several different colors, draw a few S-shaped lines, zigzags, and swirls starting at the top of your nail and heading toward the tip. Flip your brush over and use its tip as well as the different colors to place dots in between the funky-shaped pieces.

3 Finally, apply a top coat to your nails to seal in the design.

Shattered Nails

If you're looking for something a little edgy and cool, then this is it! Super simple to copy, this design only needs a dab of pink and gold nail polishes and some funky shapes. Don't worry if your lines aren't totally perfect—it only makes the design that much cooler!

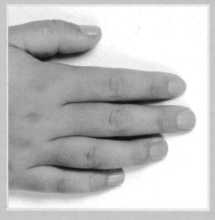

1 Start by painting your nails with a neon-pink nail polish.

2 On a cosmetic wedge, paint a wide stripe of the neon-pink polish next to a stripe of gold nail polish. Dab the cosmetic wedge onto each nail, keeping the neon pink at the cuticle to form a gradient. You may need to reapply the nail polish between nails to make the color more vibrant.

3 Using a nail art brush and black nail polish, randomly draw straight lines across the nail, making sure that some of the lines intersect to create triangle shapes.

4 Finally, apply a top coat to your nails to seal in the design.

Flip-Flop Nails

If you dream of spending your summer by the water with your toes buried in the sand, then this design is perfect for you! Try on these colorful flip-flops and you'll feel like you're at the beach again, watching the waves roll by!

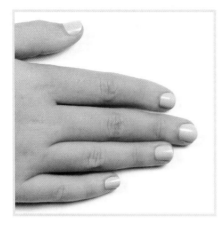

1 Start by painting your nails with a light-blue nail polish.

2 Using a nail art brush and a few brightly colored nail polishes, create the base of the flip-flop by drawing small, long oval shapes on each nail. Make sure that one end of the ovals is a bit wider than the other, as this will be where you draw your flip-flop strap.

3 Using a nail art brush and white nail polish, draw a C shape near the top of the widest part on the oval.

4 Finally, apply a top coat to your nails to seal in the design.

Frankenstein Nails

Celebrate Halloween by dressing up your nails with this electrifying design! With a few simple shapes and a dab or two of green nail polish, you'll bring this spooky monster to life in just a matter of minutes.

1 Start by painting your nails with a dark-green nail polish.

2 Using a small nail art brush and black nail polish, create a few short diagonal lines coming away from the cuticle. Fill in the area from the triangles to the cuticle with black nail polish. These should form triangle shapes for your monster's hair.

3 With a small nail art brush and black nail polish, draw a long horizontal line in the center of the nail and a shorter one right underneath, close to the nail tip.

4 Using a small dotting tool or toothpick, place two black dots along the longer line for your monster's eyes.

5 Finally, apply a top coat to your nails to seal in the design.

Be My Valentine Nails

Creating the perfect valentines may take some time with all the hole punching, cutting, and gluing, but these sure don't! You'll see that all it takes is just a few brushstrokes and some pretty nail polish to make your Valentine's Day-inspired nails really stand out. Don't be surprised if these valentines inspire others to send you their own heart-shaped creations!

1 Start by painting your nails with a light-pink nail polish.

2 Using a nail art brush and hot-pink nail polish, create two small half circles at the tip of your nail. Fill in the half circles with the hot-pink nail polish.

3 Using a dotting tool and white nail polish, place dots along the inside edge of the top of the heart.

4 Finally, apply a top coat to your nails to seal in the design.

Paw Print Nails

Whether you're a cat person or a dog lover, this design will remind you of your favorite furry friend. It's simple but fun and purr-fect for when you're missing your buddy. Your friends will definitely want to pounce on this awesome design when they see it, turning you into the cat's meow!

1   Start by painting your index- and ring-finger nails with a light-blue nail polish. Then paint the rest of your nails with a light-pink nail polish.

2   Using a dotting tool and black nail polish, place three large dots together in the shape of a Y on your index- and ring-finger nails.

3   Using the same tools, place four smaller dots around one of the larger dots.

4 Using a dotting tool and white nail polish, place dots in a polka-dot pattern on all the other nails.

5 Finally, apply a top coat to your nails to seal in the design.

Peace Sign Nails

A symbol of love and harmony, the peace sign has been worn by people for lots and lots of years. This nail art design is a fun and colorful way to show off your peaceful nature and kindness toward others.

1 Start by painting your nails with a hot-pink nail polish.

2 On a cosmetic wedge, paint a wide stripe of pink nail polish with stripes of orange and green nail polishes below that first stripe. Dab the cosmetic wedge onto each nail, keeping the pink at the cuticle to form a gradient. You may need to reapply the nail polish between nails to make the color more vibrant.

3 Using a nail art brush and black nail polish, draw a Y shape with a short line coming out of the middle of the Y.

4 Using the same tools, draw a circle around the shape you created.

5 Finally, apply a top coat to your nails to seal in the design.

Rainbow Glitter Nails

This bright and sparkly design will make you shine no matter where you are! Inspired by the colors of the rainbow, it goes well with just about any outfit, and you can even wear this out to parties, sleepovers, or family celebrations.

1   Start by painting your nails with a white nail polish.

2   On a cosmetic wedge, paint a wide stripe of pink nail polish next to a stripe of orange nail polish. Dab the cosmetic wedge onto your thumb nail, keeping the pink on the outside and the orange near your fingers to form a gradient. You may need to reapply the nail polish between nails to make the color more vibrant. Using rainbow-colored nail polishes and a new wedge each time, repeat this step for the remaining nails. Use orange and yellow nail polishes for your index finger, yellow and green ones for your middle finger, green and blue ones for your ring finger, and blue and purple nail polishes for your pinky finger.

3   Apply a chunky black-and-white glitter nail polish to each nail.

4   Finally, apply a top coat to your nails to seal in the design.

Santa Nails

Like many other kids, you might wait all year long for the most festive time of year. But with this design, you don't have to wait until December 25th for Santa to make his jolly appearance! Show off his cheerful face and snow-white beard all month long with this adorable nail art design!

1 Start by painting your nails with a red nail polish.

2 Using a dotting tool and white nail polish, place dots along the tips of all of the nails except the middle-finger nail. The dots should be close together and can even overlap.

3 Using a nail art brush and light-beige nail polish, draw an oval in the center of your middle-finger nail.

4 Using a dotting tool and white nail polish, place a few large dots above the circle going across the nail.

5 Using a nail art brush and white nail polish, paint around the rest of the oval to create Santa's famous beard.

6 Using a dotting tool and black nail polish, place two small dots in the center of the oval for his eyes.

7 Using the dotting tool and red nail polish, place a small dot below the eyes for his nose.

8 Finally, apply a top coat to your nails to seal in the design.

Smiley Face Nails

Say cheese! Bright and cheerful, this design is sure to keep you smiling all day long. Wear it during picture day as a reminder to ham it up for the camera, or when you're taking tests to perk up your spirits.

1 Start by painting your ring-finger nails with a yellow nail polish. Then paint the rest of your nails with a red nail polish.

2 Using a dotting tool and yellow nail polish, place dots in a polka-dot pattern on all of the red nails.

3 Using a nail art brush and black nail polish, draw two short vertical ovals right next to each other and toward the top of the nail. These will be your smiley face's eyes.

4 Using the same tools, draw a curved line just below the eyes for the mouth and a vertical line at the end of both sides of the curve.

5 Using the nail art brush and black nail polish, create a small half circle along the mouth.

6 Using the nail art brush and red nail polish, fill in the half circle with red, leaving a black border around it. This is your smiley face's tongue.

7 Finally, apply a top coat to your nails to seal in the design.

Teddy Bear Nails

Cute and cuddly, this teddy bear is ready to be your lifelong friend! You can wear this adorable design to your best friend's sleepover or create it with your pals at you very own nighttime party!

1 Start by painting your nails with a light-pink nail polish.

2 Using a nail art brush and brown nail polish, create a half circle at the tip of your ring-finger nail.

3 Using a dotting tool and brown nail polish, place one medium-size dot on top of either side of the larger circle. These will be your teddy bear's ears.

4 Using the dotting tool and white nail polish, place a dot inside of each ear.

5 Using the same tools, place dots just below the ears for eyes.

6 Using the dotting tool and black nail polish, place two smaller black dots in the eyes.

7 Using a nail art brush and white nail polish, create a small half circle at the tip of your nail.

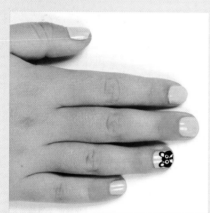

8 Using the nail art brush and black nail polish, draw a triangle for the nose and two curved lines coming out from underneath it.

9 Finally, apply a top coat to your nails to seal in the design.

Two-Colored Dots Nails

Simple but cool, this nail art design is perfect for beginners! All you need is two of your favorite colored nail polishes and a couple of easy-to-use tools. After just a few dots and dabs of nail polish, you've got a really fun design you can show off to friends!

1 Start by painting your nails with a light-pink nail polish.

2 Using a nail art brush and a purple nail polish, draw a diagonal line across your nails and fill in the bottom section with the nail polish.

3 Using a dotting tool and the purple nail polish, place dots on the top section of the nail along the diagonal.

4 Using a dotting tool and the pink nail polish, place dots on the bottom section of the nail along the diagonal.

5 Finally, apply a top coat to your nails to seal in the design.

Valentine's Day Nails

This pretty design may just become one of your favorite Valentine's Day creations! It may not be as sweet as candy or as crafty as a homemade card, but its bright colors and punch-out holes will remind you of your favorite valentines and what makes the day so fun!

1 Start by painting your nails with a red nail polish.

2 Using a dotting tool and white nail polish, place a curved row of dots in the center of your nail.

3 Using a nail art brush and white nail polish, fill in the area from the row to your cuticle.

4 Using the dotting tool and the red nail polish, place dots inside the white ones you first created.

5 Finally, apply a top coat to your nails to seal in the design.

Watermelon Nails

Take a bite out of this juicy watermelon design! So bright and tasty, it looks real enough to nibble on!

1 Start by painting your nails with a medium-pink nail polish.

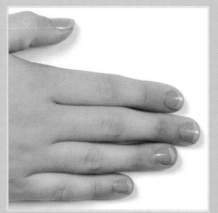

2 Using a nail art brush and green nail polish, create a French tip by drawing a thick curved line near the tip of your nail and fill in the area from the line to the nail tip.

3 Using the nail art brush and white nail polish, draw a curved line right above the green tip.

4 Using the nail art brush and dark-green nail polish, draw thin vertical lines over the green tip to make a more realistic-looking watermelon.

5 Using the nail art brush and black nail polish, draw teardrop shapes for seeds right above the white curved line.

6 Finally, apply a top coat to your nails to seal in the design.

Haunted House Nails

Ever wish you could figure out what goes bump in the night? With this haunting design, you can imagine all the possibilities as you create your very own haunted house! While you'll never have to worry about watching your step as you walk into this old, spooky house, it'll still be fun picturing all the ghouls that could be hiding inside!

1 Start by painting your nails with a dark-purple nail polish.

2 Using a nail art brush and a pale-yellow nail polish, draw a small circle for the moon ⅔ of the way from the nail tip on the middle finger.

3 Using the nail art brush and black nail polish, draw a square at the tip of the nail. Fill it in with black nail polish.

4 Using the same tools, draw a triangle just above the square to create the house's roof.

5 Using the nail art brush and pale-yellow nail polish, draw a rectangle inside the house to create a door.

6 Using the nail art brush and pale-yellow nail polish, draw a square inside the house to create a window.

7 Finally, apply a top coat to your nails to seal in the design.

Cupcake Nails

Looking for a yummy treat? This nail art is perfect for anyone with a sweet tooth. Filled with colorful sprinkles and tons of gooey frosting, you'll love creating this tasty design!

1 Start by painting your nails with a dark-purple nail polish.

2 Using a nail art brush and light-pink nail polish, draw a large square at the tip of each nail. The square should go about ⅓ up the nail.

3 Using the nail art brush and a dark-pink nail polish, draw thin vertical lines on the light-pink area.

4 Using a dotting tool and white nail polish, place a line of large dots along the edge of the square for the cupcake's frosting.

5 Using a dotting tool and different nail polish colors, randomly place small dots in the white area to create sprinkles.

6 Finally, apply a top coat to your nails to seal in the design.

Canadian Flag Nails

O Canada, how we love thee! Whether you're from the country or just can't get enough of Canadians like Justin Bieber and Ryan Gosling, this design is sure to reveal your passion.

1 Start by painting your thumb, middle-, and pinky-finger nails with a white nail polish. Then paint the rest of your nails with a red nail polish.

2 Using a nail art brush and red nail polish, draw a vertical line in the center of your middle-finger nail. Then draw a V shape that intersects the line in the middle.

3 Using the same tools, draw two more lines coming out from the top three lines you already drew. The line closest to the tip should be left untouched.

4 Using the same tools, draw curved lines to connect the existing lines and create the shape of a maple leaf. Fill in the leaf with the red nail polish.

5 Finally, apply a top coat to your nails to seal in the design.

Union Jack Nails

If you've ever dreamed of taking a spin on the London Eye or listening to Big Ben's ring, you'll absolutely fall in love with this UK-inspired nail art! Perfect for Brits and non-Brits alike, this cool design shows off the United Kingdom's national flag, which is also known as the Union Jack.

1   Start by painting your nails with a dark-blue nail polish.

2   Using a nail art brush and white nail polish, draw a thick cross shape on the ring-finger nail. Then draw a thick X shape that overlaps the cross shape.

3   Using the nail art brush and red nail polish, draw a thin X shape inside of the original X, so that it leaves a white border.

4 Using the nail art brush and red nail polish, draw a thin cross inside of the original white cross, leaving a white border.

5 Finally, apply a top coat to your nails to seal in the design.

ACKNOWLEDGMENTS

Thank you to all my friends and family who have always been there to support me. I would also like to give a big thanks to everyone at Adams Media for giving me another opportunity to show off my nail art designs and to our awesome hand models Annie, Audrey, Caroline, Danica, Emma, Josie, Kathryn, Norah, Maria, and Sadie for being a part of our photo shoot. And last but certainly not least, I want to say thank you to all of the people who have watched my YouTube videos throughout the years; I would never have had this amazing opportunity without your continued support.